Customer Service Excellence:
Blocking & Tackling Tips for Managers/Supervisors of Front Line Employees

Ray Roberge

Foreword

I was once involved in a very successful company turnaround. When peers asked how we did it, I told them that there was no one silver bullet, but a thousand different little things. This book demonstrates how many little things result in great successes. *Customer Service Excellence: Blocking & Tackling Tips for Managers/Supervisors of Front Line Employees* is the culmination of twenty-plus years of successful customer service support and management by an exceptional manager and department leader. The insights provided in this methodical memoir of Ray Roberge will enlighten and enhance the perspectives of even the most seasoned professional. Whether looking for a guide to manage your first assignment, revitalize a stressed department or enhance an existing operation, this book provides meaningful, experienced based insights for customer service professionals at all levels.

The following pages provide a systematic approach to recognize and implement practices that are theoretically based and universally recognized fundamentals for exceptional customer support through stories of personal experiences and effective program implementations. The book focuses on employee involvement, customer relationships, self-efficacy and autonomy to empower all parties to achieve a level of satisfaction, which exceeds that provided by many support functions.

The overall message that resounds throughout these pages demonstrates how allowing service personnel the ability to make decisions, execute problem solving measures, and become empowered result in a lasting feeling of satisfaction, belonging and enhanced dedication of the team. Customer service professionals will benefit from reading this book by recognizing existing disconnects within a department and applying the solutions recommended. The book provides techniques to:

- Involve employees
- Empower employees
- Avert disasters

- Improve customer relations
- Manage upward
- Reduce costs
- Improve efficiencies
- Provide exceptional support
- Enhance firm image

Ray Roberge has an extremely successful record of department management, revitalizing teams, improving efficiencies, reducing employee turnover, and lowering costs. The departments he has managed are the recipients on countless Customer Satisfaction Awards from both industry organizations as well as J.D. Power and Associates.

This book will benefit seasoned managers, managers facing organizational distress or organizational change, or reorganization issues. Regardless of the size of the firm or size of the department, the advice contained in these pages is immutable and will benefit any organization. Consuming the wisdom and experiences presented in this book are sure to provide new insights and rejuvenate motivations to enhance even the best-oiled Customer Service Department. It is well-written and easy to digest. Every page is crammed full of useful hints and tips so that you can profit from them.

Dr. Robert W. Reich, DBA
Assistant Professor of Management
Lynn University
Boca Raton, Florida

Table of Contents

Preface

Customer service is a topic that is talked about endlessly when it comes to the success of a company. In my more than 20 years of experience in customer service and support departments, I have found that customer service is vastly misunderstood or misquoted for many reasons.

Companies spend millions of dollars annually trying to crack the code to excellent customer service, but many times they are looking in the wrong place or think there is a magic formula from some consulting firm. Many times they look for the answer externally while internal company activities are overlooked.

Excellent customer service is always expected in the luxury product industry. However, there is a preconceived notion that poor customer service is found in more competitive products. This is purely a myth. It is possible to have great customer service and be very price competitive.

Let's talk about employees for a moment. Those who see their job strictly as a paycheck are not committed to their employer and do not exhibit the tendencies for excellent customer service. The employee who feels like a number has no loyalty to the company. The company is merely a vehicle to feed their family, give them spending money for their time off, or ultimately get them to their next job. It is no harder to treat your employees in a positive manner, creating happy employees, than it is to treat them poorly, creating employees who see their job merely as a paycheck.

I was recently a guest speaker at a university, and the director of the MBA program asked me if "things had changed out there in the industry". When I inquired about what he meant, he asked how I managed customer service or groups of employees differently today compared to years past. I told him that I do virtually the same things everywhere I go, in all industries, and it continues to be extremely successful. After having this discussion, I started thinking about what I do and why I have had success in so many different places. The truth is that I always start out with the basics and build on them.

So after working in multiple industries for more than 20 years and finding that no industry was better than any other at customer service, I would like to share my techniques to create excellent customer service and loyal employees. I have used the same techniques over and over in multiple industries and they have worked every time with all levels of employees. I call it the **Blocking and Tackling Techniques to Customer Service Excellence**!

Let's get started.

1.

Mission/Vision Statements – Relate Them to Your Employees' Responsibilities

Corporate Vision/Mission statements sound great when you read them, but how do you translate them to your front line employees? Let's look at a few examples.

Corporation A:

Corporation A will operate and lead the world's best-known, most profitable recreation and lifestyle brands. We won't be satisfied until we've redefined marine, recreation and wellness experiences for generations to come. By leveraging our expertise and passion for innovation, we'll create the most coveted products and experiences for fun- and fitness-seekers all over the world—with the goal of helping people live life well.

The average employee who earns $30,000 per year has no idea how their job relates to being the world's best-known, most profitable recreation and lifestyle brands. One simple reason is that the majority of these employees cannot afford the products that Corporation A produces in its factories whether it is a $2,000 piece of equipment or a million dollar vehicle. Most employees have obligations, such as raising a family, or other responsibilities that need their hard earned money. This is where corporations fall down. They assume that the employee is on board with the mission and has a vested interest; however, most employees have no clue what the mission is and, quite frankly, have no vested interest at all. They feel they are like a hamster on a wheel that gets the executives their big paycheck/bonus and shareholders their return on investment.

Corporation B:

Our vision is to be viewed as the best specialty chemical company in the world.

Our Mission: Why We Are Here
We satisfy our customers by delivering results through quality chemical products and services. Our desire to grow drives our passion to win in the marketplace. With a unified, low-cost operating structure, we'll remain competitive across every business and in every geographic region.

What does it take to be the "best specialty chemical company in the world"? Is that my job or is there someone in another facility that makes this happen? Whose responsibility is it to "drive our passion to win in the marketplace"? Corporation B makes chemicals for goodness sake! Chemicals in a barrel or container are not exciting or sexy. These are the kinds of thoughts you are dealing with. It is your job to change the mindset of these employees and make them dedicated loyal employees who care about the success of the company for the right reasons. Whether an employee spends two years or 20 years with the company, it is up to the managers and supervisors to keep them energized and productive at all levels.

Let's start at the beginning. What are the employees' job responsibilities? We'll start with a few examples.

Customer Service – Customer Service has many roles depending on the company. Many customer service departments deal with order entry as well as answering questions from customers about their orders. Let's break down a few elements for order entry.

1. Customers expect their orders to be entered the same day or at least within 24 business hours. Many customers like confirmation that their order was received and processed. The customer service associate can help the company become the most profitable by ensuring the order is entered as stated (i.e. 100% accurate). Mistakes cost both the company and the customer money. The customers are inconvenienced because they have to deal with credits and discrepancies, and they are often passed from person to person to fix the problem. If a customer service associate

has a question about the order, they need to make contact with the customer to verify that the information is correct. Customers appreciate the attention to detail.

2. Was the order filled completely? This could be critical to a customer being able to keep their own assembly line open, satisfying one of their own customers or making a deadline. If it is not possible to fill the order completely or the customer will not receive the product in the time they requested, it is time to contact the customer to discuss what can be provided and what cannot. What you may think is no big deal maybe a very big deal to the customer. **Do not assume!! Make the call!!**

Technical Support – Technical Support's typical role is to assist a customer with a technical question about a product or to assist with the installation of a product. Many customers do not wish to read instructions; they prefer to call for help. So what are some elements customers are looking for that would help your company become the best in the world?

1. When a customer calls technical support, they are expecting the person on the other end of the line to be an expert on the product or service. The technical support associate needs to understand the importance of providing accurate information. It is important for the associate to have this information handy, whether it's electronic or hard copy, to quickly assist the customer. Time is money, and customers will purchase products where support is accurate, efficient and easy to access. If the tech support agent doesn't know the answer, he or she should tell the caller that he or she will find the answer and call the customer back. At that point, the tech support agent should suggest and confirm a convenient time to call the customer back. Follow- up on or before the agreed on time is critical. This can make or break the confidence the customer has in the company. If the caller needs an immediate answer, ask politely if they can wait while an answer is researched.

2. One way to show Technical Support associates that the company cares about them is to provide ongoing training for products and services. Far too often training is offered only once, and the company thinks that is enough. False! Give associates a chance to use the product or observe it being made. Task them with becoming a subject matter expert on a particular product. This gives them ownership and a sense of pride.

3. Make sure the employee knows exactly what is expected to perform the job. This means going over each duty required for their position. The good news is that breaking down the responsibilities of someone's job works in any department. Make sure the employee knows the importance of each task. If you never tell an individual what they are doing is important, they won't think it is important either. Always try to relate it to the fact that we are all customers at some point; remember how we feel when we are disappointed with a product we purchased or our order was mishandled. This is not the memory we want for our customers. Remind them to take the extra step to make sure the customer is pleased with their service.

Tip # 1

Don't Assume! Ask the employee if they understand their job or if they have any questions! Employees appreciate the fact that you have an interest in their job. Relate the elements of the employee's job responsibilities to how it will make your company "The Best in the World".

"If your employees know you care, they will work harder to do a great job"

2.

Phone Etiquette – Make It a Priority!

Studies have shown that visual effects, such as facial expression and body language, account for more than 70% of positive interactions with a customer. We all know that we cannot meet with every customer in person; hence we have customer service and support services via 1-800 numbers, chat, email etc. This automatically puts your employee at a disadvantage because without the facial expressions and body language, the customer can be offended if they believe they are being disrespected or ignored.

How associates answer the phone and handle customers has been overlooked in many organizations. Customers are most likely calling because they have a problem. If the associate seems to show no interest, that customer can't wait to unleash their wrath and take out their frustration. If your associate responds with frustration or lack of interest, the customer will not be happy and will leave the call unsatisfied even if his issues are ultimately resolved. We will talk about ways to diffuse customer anger in a later chapter, but let's focus on phone etiquette for now.

It is difficult for a customer to get angry when a pleasant voice answers the phone and is interested in resolving their problem. Customers are generally surprised when they call a 1-800 number and the voice on the other end is genuinely interested in helping them solve their problem. This is the beginning of a successful phone interaction and will lead to "First Call Resolution" and a happy customer which is very important for your organization.

Training and monitoring are the keys to improving your team's phone etiquette skills. This section is talking about focusing on phone calls, but it also applies to chat, email and any way companies interact with customers. Your employees will say that they know how to answer the phone, but in my many years of walking around and listening to calls there is always room for improvement. Supervisors and Managers need to take the lead on this one. You can learn through training as well. Employees are very sensitive to the "Do as I say Not as I do" actions and will be more than happy to point it out to you if you are caught with poor phone skills.

Phone etiquette training should not be limited to customer service or technical support departments. One of the most overlooked positions is the receptionist or operator that directs calls throughout the organization. Whether you realize it or not, your receptionist or operator represents your company far more often than any other individual because they potentially handle every call that comes into the company. I have actually worked at companies where the receptionist was the person that "could not make it" at any other position. Bad choice!!! We will discuss these positions later as well.

No matter how good you think your team's phone skills are, continuous phone training is key. Phone etiquette requires constant reminders of the proper phone techniques so people do not fall back into bad habits.

I recommend your staff have some sort of training at least monthly. There are many tools and educational videos out there. I recommend a program that uses15- to 30- minute training sessions. The training typically discusses one technique at a time so it is not a huge time draw on your team.

One series I use is the *"Telephone Doctor"* by Nancy Friedman. I have used her series for more than 15 years, and it has worked every time in various industries. The multiple DVD training series comes with workbooks and Power Point slides to administer the training. Each DVD takes 12 to 30 minutes to administer. They may be somewhat corny by filmmakers' standards, but they are very effective in getting the technique across to the trainees.

I started using the series again about two years ago when I joined a new company. I was sensitive to the fact many of the employees were long-term employees and they would laugh at the idea of doing phone etiquette training. Much to my surprise, the training was received with enthusiasm and people expressed their thanks for providing the training. We now provide monthly training sessions for each department. The bottom line for me is that this series works. There are many other tools out there, so pick the one that works for your team.

After 16 months and seven training DVD's, our customers are received by much happier employees with a consistent message when they call for assistance with our products. The general response I get from employees is that the training is a great reminder of how to treat customers the correct way to create customer loyalty. Our Voice of Customer (VOC) surveys are validating this statement. We will discuss this topic later in the book as well.

Note: I am not affiliated with the *Telephone Doctor* and receive no compensation for mentioning them in this chapter. I just like the series.

Another item that may work is a phone tip card. The card has a series of tips that the employee can refer to as they are talking to a customer to make sure that they ask all the right questions and all topics are covered. It doesn't have to be fancy, just functional.

Tip # 2

1. Continuous training is critical to sustaining good phone habits. Short, focused training sessions keep training manageable and will keep your team energized. The best part is that your customers will have a superior experience which creates a positive work environment and happy customers.

2. Ask your employees to assist in the training and developing the training material. They may surprise you!!

"Catch your people doing it Right! They will continue to shine for you!"

3.

Employee Empowerment – Reality or Myth?

When I ask employees if they are empowered, they frequently and emphatically answer yes. Unfortunately, I typically find out later that the employees are only empowered slightly if at all. In many organizations, the supervisors or managers hold all the power. The associates under them don't make many decisions at all without getting the boss's approval. It is a way for the boss to hold the power and work to prove his worth to the team and the senior managers. However, if the boss is on vacation or is unavailable, nothing gets accomplished. This, folks, is not empowerment! It is gridlock!

Employees are not empowered if they have to ask someone above them for approval for every exception they encounter in their jobs. If a customer service associate is helping a customer that has ordered a product that is out of stock and the employee cannot make a substitution (with the customer's approval of course), they are not empowered. If a technical support person does not have the authority to assist a customer by providing a replacement part at no charge, they are not empowered.

Typical Situation

Unfortunately, not all employees want to be empowered because they are afraid of doing something wrong and getting into trouble. Management drives the culture for empowerment or lack thereof. If managers and supervisors set the tone that employees will be disciplined if they make a mistake, the employees will be more than happy to sit back and let someone else make the decisions. This does not drive development of your front line employees. The only purpose it serves is creating a line at the boss's door waiting for him or her to make a decision.

Over time the managers will start to feel resentment or overworked because every employee is pulling on them for a

9

decision for even the simplest things. As workloads increase, it is critical that the manager recognize the need to get his employees involved and start to allow them to make some of the front line decisions to keep work flow efficient and moving.

Let's discuss some ways to make empowerment a reality.

One of the first things I like to do is meet with my new group and ask them if they are empowered to make decisions. If the answer is yes, I like to ask what type of situations they encounter and what decisions are they allowed to make. When I took responsibility of a group a few years ago I did this and the group claimed that they had the power. Unfortunately, I never followed up to ask what types of decisions they typically make. I quickly found out that they made only limited decisions, which affected our business by losing potential selling opportunities. A customer called in for a product that we were out of at the time and production of the product was not scheduled to resume for more than a week. The customer service associate told the customer that we did not have it in stock and that it was going to be at least a week until it was available. The customer chose not to order. I got a call from our salesman and he was not happy that the customer went elsewhere. When I checked on the situation, I found that we had a similar product that we could have substituted, but the employee didn't offer it to the customer. When I asked the employee why they didn't offer a substitute, I was told that they did not have the authority to offer a substitution or upgrade. I knew we had work to do!

At this point, I took the opportunity to implement some policies that allowed the customer service associate to offer substitutions. The new policy gave the customer associate the authority to offer a substitute at the same price of the originally requested product if the price difference was not greater than 5 percent. I also allowed the employees to offer an upgraded product to the customer at a 5 percent discount to give the customer another option. The first thing I heard from my employees is "We have never been able to do that before."

Here are a couple of things that managers and supervisors need to realize:

1.   Empowering your employees doesn't make your position less important. You shouldn't be thinking "my boss won't need me if my employees can make the decisions". Empowering your employees allows you as a manager to do other things to help your company. Thus it makes you more valuable to your senior managers and to your employees. You will be free to take on more responsibility in the company. If you are not growing, you are falling behind the competition.

2.   By having more time to review what your group is doing, you can start to develop a bigger picture for your group which will make your group more valuable. You need to take yourself out of the day-to-day duties from time to time to evaluate things that could make your group even more efficient. I call this "staring out the window." I like to stare out the window and think about how I can help my group improve. A few years ago, I had a wonderful second floor office that overlooked a field where deer came out to play during the day. I used to come up with some great ideas as I watched out the window. People would come by from time to time and say "What are you doing? Wasting time?" I would tell them "No, I'm thinking about the next step we need to take to improve and out-work our competition". People laughed, but they would come to see me if they needed to resolve a problem and sometimes we would stare out the window to solve it!

3.   Customers love it when the person answering the phone can solve their problem or give them options. If the customer feels that the front line employee can't make a decision, the call will be escalated to you, and before you know it you will be solving customer issues more often than you would care to admit. Think of it this way: The higher the customer has to go to get resolution, the more it costs your company. Whether it is time or additional compensation to the customer, it costs more money. I always tell my employees "the higher the customer goes, the more is costs to resolve." Solve problems at the lowest level. The customer is happier and the company wins.

Tip # 3

Your value is not based on your making all the decisions. Your value is empowering your employees to make the front line decisions. That way you can make higher-level decisions to keep your company in front of the competition. Empowering your employees is a huge step in the development of future supervisors and managers. Set guidelines and rules for your employees and unleash their power.

4.

Receptionists/Operators –
How Critical Are They?

When you ask senior managers or executives which of their employees talk to the customer most, many would say their sales people. I would say in general that is incorrect. The person directing all the calls coming into the company talks to the customer the most. If you have an automated system, don't think you are immune from this issue either. Your automated system can actually drive customers away if it is set up incorrectly.

In some organizations, the receptionist has been the person who couldn't make it anywhere else. The company decided to keep this individual for some unknown reason and tolerated the indifference. The motto was "well they are just answering the phone". **Just answering the phone. Yikes!**

This person is the first interaction that a customer or potential customer has with your company. You want a person that has energy and a pleasant voice that represents your company well. The receptionist/operator most likely talks to more customers than your best salesman. This position is important and it should be treated that way. You can utilize this person for other duties while they are not on the phone. This person should also be part of the regular phone training discussed in chapter 2.

Let me put it this way. How do you feel when you call a company and the person who first answers the phone is rude, indifferent or just plain unhelpful. Does it make you want to keep doing business with that company?

Many companies have gone to automated phone systems and have eliminated the receptionist position. This is fine, but be careful not to put your customer through automation hell. You need to routinely call your own company number to ensure your telephone system is working as designed. It is embarrassing when a customer has to send you an email or call you on your cell phone to tell you your phone system is not working. Be sensitive to customer visits and how they are going to get in touch with you when they arrive at your place of business. Give them your cell number or set up a way to make contact so they are not left wondering how they are going to make contact after traveling to have a meeting.

Here are a few things you can do to enhance a customer's experience:

1.   It really goes back to Chapter 1 in the fact that you need to make sure the employee knows how important the position is. This is sometimes hard to convey because it is usually not a high-paying position, but it is worth the time to make the effort.

2.   Ensure that the person gets training on a regular basis. Even if they do not work for you, offer the training to that person's supervisor. Good habits will rub off.

What if your system is automated?

1.   Call your own number or work with the person responsible for the phones to understand the phone logic and what a customer has to go through to connect with the person they are calling. If it is too difficult, work to make it more streamlined. Offer an option to dial an extension early in the process if they can't call you directly.

2.   Have the most popular options that a customer is looking for early in the phone decision tree so a customer doesn't have to listen to 30 seconds of nonsense before they hear what they want to make the connection.
3.   Offer a phone directory so they can search for the person they are calling by name.

Tip #4

1. Realize the importance of this position and make sure your employee knows how important it is as well.
2. For automated systems, make them as simple as possible and offer a contact list early on in the automation process.

5.

Turning Customer Service Employees into Sales People

Are some of your best sales people in customer service? If they are, congratulations! You have unlocked the power of customer service as an extension of the sales department. Many companies fail to utilize these talented people. Think about it this way: customer service has to know your product line well to be able to enter orders and also discuss the product with customers. Who talks to the customer as much or more than the sales department? You guessed it – Customer Service!

I stand by this statement - **"Sales sells the first one, but Customer Service sells the Rest!"**

This statement holds true for all the support services whether it be technical support, parts or other departments that support the customer. In my time leading support groups, I can emphatically say we sold millions of dollars' worth of product. How do I know? We tracked and published it if we could definitely tie it back to a person in the support department.

Let me give you an example: It started for me back in the 1990's when I managed a customer service group for a large chemical company. We sold commodity chemicals as well as specialty items. The plant manager used to come to me every so often and say that he needed to sell five tanker loads of a particular chemical because he had a rail car showing up in a few days and he needed the storage space. I would get my customer service group together and have them start calling customers that used that particular material. Usually within in the next 4 to 6 hours, orders were in hand and the plant manager was asking me to stop because we were going to run out before the next shipment arrived.

Many times customers have great relationships with support employees and trust them deeply. Customers sometimes think that a sales person is selling them something they don't need, or are trying to make a sales goal for their commission. Since support employees don't benefit directly through commissions, it takes the pressure off giving an opinion about a product. Most support departments are looked at strictly as a cost center which is not true when they are given the chance to expand into sales.

In my opinion, support service departments are the last to grow when business is good and the first to go when business goes flat or retracts. Unfortunately, when business starts to flatten out or shrink, customers are looking for even better support; the customer base of the current product in the field doesn't go away overnight. I fully understand that at some point a department may need to be resized to be in line with ongoing business. As each group is adjusted for size, be very careful not to always subtract from the same group.

Back to selling! Let's discuss ways to activate your customer service department into a silent selling machine. Again, technical support and other support groups can also play a critical role to increase sales.

First off, you need to convince your support people that they can sell product. Many feel they are just in clerical jobs taking orders or answering complaints. This is so far from the truth. You have to get out of the cost center mentality and turn your groups into a profit center. Whether you actually do this via a Profit & Loss statement or not doesn't matter. It is the attitude and energy that gets people excited about doing their job. Make a game out of the task with prizes and monetary rewards. The good news is that these prizes and rewards don't have to be huge to get people motivated to play.

1. Training is a big piece of selling product. If the employee does not feel comfortable talking about the features of the product they will not push it. Let the employees know that they don't have to be the experts; they just need to be able to talk about it.
2. Team the customer service employees with inside sales people or the outside sales team to generate a friendly

competitive environment. This is an opportunity for a contest.

3. Start the team out by having them suggest promotional items that already have information available, such as a sales flyer. They can send it to the person via email. Slowly the team gains knowledge of your full product line and gets the much-needed confidence to talk about products with the customers.

4. Pick things that are easy to sell to get your people in the habit of asking for add-on sales. If a customer calls and orders one product and you know they order several others from you, occasionally ask if they need to reorder the other items. You would be surprised how many times customers will check and add on product. The customer also appreciates the fact that you know their account well enough to ask about the other items they may need. You may keep the purchasing agent out of a bind.

5. Catch your employee's doing it right. Provide positive feedback and constructive criticism to encourage them to improve.

6. Find an easy way to track their success. Employees love being recognized for their talents. Tracking success also helps if you are looking to grow your department as your business grows. This shows senior management that you are paying attention. In the end it will bring bigger opportunities your way as a manager as well.

Tip #5

1. All of your employees can sell. Unleash their power to grow your business.

2. Create ways to make your employees want to sell and make it fun. The results may start out small, but will add to the bottom line.

6.

The Power of Follow-Up

This is an obvious one, but many times it is overlooked or dreaded, particularly if you are dealing with a negative situation. The crazy thing is whether it is good news or bad news, in the end, the customer appreciates the follow-up. They may be upset by the news, but at least they know the latest status of their order or the situation.

When I first started in customer service and sales, I loved being the one to relay good news! Delivering good news felt great and I couldn't wait to get the customer on the phone. But I hated to be the one delivering bad news so I would put off calling customers with bad news until I really had to make the call. No one likes getting bad news, but it is even worse if the bad news is late, and it is unacceptable when the customer has to call and track you down to get it.

Though you never know how the customer is going to react, there are things the associate can do to lessen the blow of bad news. The following things will soften bad news:

1. Call the customer as soon as possible once there is bad news to deliver. Make sure the representative has all the facts regarding the situation before making the call.
2. Let the customer know if there is a chance that the situation may change, and give them a time to expect a call back with an update.
3. Determine whether there is anything that can be done to accommodate the customer for the inconvenience even if it is not the company's fault. We'll talk more about this in the next chapter when we talk about options.

4. Always be empathetic to the customer. The customer will know if the service representative is sincere about helping them.

5. Always verify that the customer does not have any questions about the information provided to them, and let them know that representatives are available if they think of questions in the future.

Procrastinating doesn't make the bad news go away. It usually makes it worse. If there is no set time for representatives to call the customers back, it would be a good idea to block out a period of time every day to make these types of calls. It is preferable to plan for late morning or early afternoon. The end of the day is too late for the customer to make other plans, and limits what they can do before things close for the day. Another idea is to make an unpleasant call after completing a great call. This way the representative is feeling good and that positive attitude will project over the phone.

Being good at delivering bad news doesn't mean you have to like it, but it does mean you have figured out a way to help customers to the best of your ability. Again customers know when you have actually tried and they know when you are paying them lip service. Here are some things to do to be prepared for this part of the job.

1. Make sure all the information is correct and up to date. But if you have promised the customer a call and don't have all the answers yet, make the call and let the customer know where you are with their issue.

2. Don't be in a hurry. Like trying to squeeze a bad call in before a meeting or lunch. Make sure there is time to deliver the message and let the customer ask questions. If you sense that the customer will have more questions, offer to call them back later.

3. Empathize with the customer and the situation, but keep in mind what the limits are for any offers or promises.

4. Set a certain time of the day aside for these types of calls if this makes sense for the type of work that you do.

5. If you know that there is nothing more you can do for the customer, be honest and let them know that. Customers do not like to be sent down a path that leads to a dead end. They would rather know sooner than later- even if you know they will get angry.

6. Keep notes about the call if you have a Customer Relationship Management (CRM) system. If someone else on your team gets a future call they will have the information available for reference. If you do not have an electronic CRM system, keep notes in a notebook or note pad. The important thing here is to document! I would recommend that you brain storm with your team to work on these types of calls. The more you work with your group, the better they will become at handling these tough calls.

Tip #6

1. Work with your team and develop a checklist of helpful hints to handle difficult calls.
2. Great follow-up creates loyal customers!!

7.

Options/Options/Options

Have you ever called a company for help and all you got was "Sorry I can't help you" or "That is not our policy"? Many companies lose customers because they do not give their employees the ability to work outside the rules when an exception needs to be made. No company makes the perfect product all the time. Great companies empower their employees to make exceptions to take care of the customer when something goes wrong whether it is with a product or a service. These companies consider this a worthwhile expense and part of doing business.

Customers like options when they have had a bad experience. If you have a bad meal at a restaurant many places will compensate you for the meal, provide you with a free dessert or give you a voucher for the next visit. A goodwill gesture is offered to get you to come back because they care about your experience.

Companies typically allocate money to what they call "customer goodwill" or "customer accommodation". The money is to be used when a customer has had a poor experience with your product or service. The goal of this pool of money is to win the customer back. It costs much more to get a customer back after you lose them than to pay the small amount to make them happy.

Treat your customer as you would like to be treated. If you had a problem with a product you purchased, how would you feel if all you heard was "No, no, no. Can't help you"?

When I worked in the marine industry our product had a one year bow to stern warranty. This was great for people in the south who could use their boat year round, but did not work so well for customers who lived in the north that purchased their boat during the fall and did not use it until the spring of the next year. So, in essence they only really got a 3 to 4 month warranty. We routinely received calls from customers for small issues that would arise during the first few months they used the boat after spending most of the year in storage.

My team would take into consideration the nature of the issue to see if we could help the customer. We routinely offered the part at a discount or offered to replace it free of charge if the customer paid the labor charge. We offered options to the customer that did not always include getting things for free.

Many times the customer was willing to pay his share and appreciated the fact that we offered something to assist. Some customers want everything for free. I'm here to tell you it is hard to win with this type of customer, but you have to make the best decision for each situation. We did not help all customers, but we helped many and it paid off in customer loyalty. Many of our customers started out buying $20,000 boats and 10 years later were buying $250,000 boats with numerous boats in between.

In contrast, I worked in another industry for a time and ran into a technical support/warranty manager that boasted that his customer goodwill was zero. He did not work for me at the time so I asked him if he felt good about that. He quickly stated, 'Yes I do". My office was next to the technical support & warranty group that this manager ran. I heard the technicians spend countless hours arguing with customers about how the product was out of warranty or that they must have done something wrong to cause it to break and it was not covered under warranty. Sometimes the parts we were talking about were less than $5.00 in cost to the company. If you added up the time the technician spent on the phone arguing with the customer, it cost more than the part was worth just in time spent on the phone. In addition, it created a very dissatisfied customer that was going to let their friends know how poor our service was for our products. This also created tensions with our dealers because the customer would complain to them about the service. Our dealers were not exclusive to our product so as you would expect, the dealer recommended a different product in the future.

I later took responsibility for the technical support group and we changed the policy. The employees were given rules about what they could do to satisfy the customer. In the end, the customers were much happier, the employees were much happier and our customer goodwill was less than $25,000 annually on sales of more than $50 million. This equals .05% of sales. The nasty emails about our products and policies slowly changed to emails of appreciation for our first-class customer service.

Remember, many times a customer accommodation doesn't have to cost a lot of money. It is true that it is the thought that counts in many of these situations.

Work with your team to develop potential options that works for your business.

Here are a few things that I have been able to use in the past to keep customers after a bad experience.

- Discount the replacement product that they are purchasing.
- If your product has a warranty, extend the warranty for the customer or provide an extended warranty.
- Offer to upgrade the product at no extra charge.
- Offer to overnight the package if for some reason the part was delayed at no fault of the customer.
- Provide a coupon for a discount on a future purchase.

My experience shows that the faster you can take care of the customer, the higher likelihood of the customer coming back. Studies have shown that a customer who has a problem resolved quickly and fairly has more loyalty than one that has never had a problem at all.

As stated in an earlier chapter - "**Sales sells the first one! Service sells the rest!**" I stand by this and have had many conversations with sales people to defend it, and I truly believe this to be true over and over again no matter what the product or service.

Tip #7

The more quickly you handle the situation, the cheaper it is for the company and the customer is happier. If you frustrate and dissatisfy the customer and then give in later, the customer will still be unhappy with your company overall. So even though the customer got what they wanted in the end, they will still feel like you tried to cheat them out of something and will pass that along to their friends.

8.

Build Processes – Don't Allow Tribal Knowledge to Prevail

Tribal knowledge is defined as company knowledge that is held by an individual or a small group but is undocumented. It also potentially has never been validated for its accuracy. Tribal knowledge is a good or bad thing depending on whom you speak with. Employees love it because they feel like it adds value to their employment.

Managers sometimes boast about how much one of their people knows about one thing or another. If any of the above statements rings true with you, then you need to get nervous and work toward building processes. Process driven businesses will always win in the end. I had two incidents early in my career that sold me on processes.

First incident:

I worked for a large chemical company as a regional customer service manager and had been at the facility for about 2 years. The facility was one of the company's largest distribution warehouses and it also housed the purchasing group. The manager of the purchasing group was an old pro at purchasing. He had been in the industry for more than 20 years and knew everyone including competitors. He had a strong group, or so I thought at the time.

I came to work one Monday morning and it seemed like a normal day with the warehouse buzzing at 6 am with trucks running in and out. Forklifts were scurrying about with drums on the forks like ants gathering food for the colony. All seemed normal until my boss called me into his office with a concerned look on his face. His concerned look soon became my disbelief. He informed me that the purchasing manager had died unexpectedly over the weekend and that he needed me to manage the purchasing group until a replacement could be found.

The purchasing manager was young and seemed in good health, so it was a surprise to everyone. All I knew was that now I was responsible for an additional group of eight people that worked in a department that I knew little about. I would also soon find out that the manager took care of everything; if his team had an issue he would take care of it. I was lucky enough to find one employee that had been around a long time and she knew a lot about the day-to-day issues. She was extremely helpful as we started to put processes and policies in place to manage the daily tasks. She had no idea how much she saved me from running out of the building with my hair on fire. I later nominated her for an award, though she maintained that she was only doing her job. That may be true, but she saved this young manager and made me very successful.

Second incident:

I worked in the financial industry for a company that was working on recovering from near bankruptcy, which was a long and tedious journey.

After being in this position for about two months, I came into work one morning to find my phone message light blinking. The message was from one of my best employees and it stated to the best that I can remember:

"Ray this is Julie*, I will not be at work tomorrow and will not be coming back at all. I have left the state. Talk to Kim* and she will fill you in. She will pick up my last check and have it sent to me."

End of message. I sat in my chair and played the message over a few times just stunned at what I heard. I had a million questions, but could only wait for Kim to come to work before I got the rest of the story. Finally, she came through the door and I quickly asked her to come into my office. As it turned out, Julie was in the midst of an ugly divorce and her husband had held her and her children hostage. While the husband was in jail, Julie fled the state and I never heard from her again.

My first thought was to hope Julie and her children would be safe. Then my attention turned to how I was going to cover her work duties. I knew she had a temporary employee assisting her so I thought maybe we could hire her to take Julie's place. Boy was I wrong. The temporary employee turned out to be doing only filing and did not have the skills to take over the position. The position was critical to our operations, so panic set in because I knew from my short time there we had no processes. I would have to hope that someone else had an idea of what duties the position needed to be successful.

It took me almost a month to get things back in order. The first order of business was to get a talented person back in the position, and the next was to start cross-training to build some redundancy into the group. I found a number of positions where only one person was the expert and no one else knew exactly what they did. Much to the chagrin of these experts, I started to have them share their knowledge with other team members to head off another potential disaster. We also started to map out our processes and build regional teams to improve our performance and service to the customer.

(*True story, but I changed the names to be respectful.)

The Lessons here: Don't let a disaster catch you by surprise! Start looking at processes and develop a plan to document them today.

If you do not have many processes documented don't panic. Develop a plan to systematically start documenting what your teams do on a daily basis. I always remember my time in the Navy and how the military has done it for years. I was a Gunnery & Missile officer on a Guided Missile Destroyer, and we had standard procedures for how to do maintenance on some very complicated equipment. We could take an 18 year old sailor who had never seen a missile launcher and have him do the maintenance on the launcher because every step was documented and every tool listed. As long as he followed the process, the launcher would work and he would not have any extra parts or pieces left when he was finished.

The challenge with developing processes is that it is tedious and detailed work. You have to be very careful not to gloss over the details so your standard processes are effective. Here are some things to help you get started:

1. Get your employees involved and sell them on the benefit. The customer will get a better experience and everyday jobs will become easier, making it possible to get more accomplished in a day.
2. Start with the critical processes first. These are the ones that will slow you down or shut you down if they are not carried out on a daily basis.
3. If you have newer employees, it is sometimes good to use them because they don't bring tribal knowledge or biases to the process.
4. Convince your tribal knowledge experts that by sharing their knowledge, they become more valuable to the organization. Many times employees don't share because they feel like it gives them job security.
5. Emphasize the need to document every step of the process by position and not by a person's name. People change so a new employee may not know what Jimmy used to do, but they will know what a certain position's responsibilities are.
6. Once you have completed documenting the process, give it to an employee that has not been involved; have them go through the process to see if they get the result that the process is supposed to cover. You may laugh at this, but many times employees get confused or lost because a person that knows the process leaves steps out. The process has to be clear to make it work.
7. If the process involves a computer program, use screenshots to give employees a visual of what they should see as the process progresses. This validates that they are in the right place.
8. Keep all the processes in a common place so your employees know where to look for them.

9. Review the processes regularly because they will change as you find better ways to accomplish the work, or as your systems get updated.
10. Develop your own processes to show your employees that it is important to get these done correctly and it is important to you.

Tip #8

Processes drive improved efficiency and productivity. Sell your employees on the power of the process!

There are many names for standard processes. Use whichever one suits your situation. Some common ones include:

- Standard Operating Procedures (SOP)
- Standard Work
- Standard Work Instructions
- Best Practices

By using standard processes, the customer will get a consistent experience and your employees will be more efficient and happier.

"Tribal Knowledge only benefits the person with the knowledge! Eliminate it through process creation!"

9.

The Power of Customer Self-Service

Senior managers sometimes get nervous when you talk about providing more tools for customers to help themselves to certain information regarding your product. One contrarian belief that I have about call centers is that the goal should be to take less phone calls, not more. I always get funny looks when I say this to people. But the truth is that if your customers, particularly the Gen X and Millennials can get the information when they want it, they will be more inclined to use your product. Of course, I don't want to run call centers out of business, but it can allow your employees to focus on resolving the more complex issues that bring customers more value than sending emails with literature attachments.

Now, of course, there shouldn't be company secrets or plans on public websites, but if there is information that is sent to customers when they call, why not put it out there on your website? News Flash! Things such as sales literature and owner's manuals are already posted on blogs or message boards. You can check your competitors to see what they are doing on their sites and then check with your own customers and see what they like about your site compared to competitors' sites. Customers will typically be honest regarding this subject because if it will save them time, they will share what they would like from you as a support organization.

When I was in the marine industry, the company I was with had been in business for close to 50 years. We built great boats, so people held on to them for a long time and they were very proud of their boats. This created a dilemma for me as a support service leader. Thirty-five percent of our callers requested specification sheets or old owner's manuals for boats that were 20 to 30 years old. A customer had purchased the used boat from someone and wanted to know what the original equipment was on the boat or if we had an owner's manual for the boat. As luck would have it, we did have all the information that people were looking for, but from a company standpoint these customers were not the ones generating current revenue, so it was a drain on how we supported our current customers. The other drain was the fact that we were printing the documents and mailing them, which turned out to be a significant cost because of the large number of requests.

After doing some investigation and problem-solving exercises, we determined that it would be cost effective to have all these old documents scanned and loaded onto our website under an archive section to assist our customers.   Scanning and posting the documents it did two things: It gave owners of these old boats 24/7 access to information they never had before, and better yet, they could print whatever they wanted or just look at it online.

It also did a number of things for my team.

- Lowered our call volume by 30%
- Allowed the support representatives to guide customers to our website or email them a link to the information – Again, Options!!
- We got out of the copy & print business - a Big money saver!
- We were able to spend more time with current customers and dealers to assist with their issues so we added value to keep the company growing without adding to the headcount
- The employees were happier because they felt like their jobs became more relevant when they were busy supporting current products and engaged with new customers.

The benefits to the customer:

- 24/7 access to old information
- No waiting to get to the information. We used to mail manuals that looked horrible because we made copies and it was expensive. We did charge for the manual, but that added cost because we had to process a check. In the end we lost money.

It is important to understand the power of customer self-service. You are actually adding value instead of losing touch with the customer. It is easy to create website analytics so you can continue to fine-tune your website depending on customer patterns. It is important for your customers and your employees.

We are in the age of self-service whether it is at the gas station or the grocery store. Make it work for you. Here are some things to consider:

- Review your current website and see what self-help is available. In other words, take an inventory of what is already on your website.
- Start tracking your customer calls, and collect the most common topics.
- Ask your employees what they feel would be beneficial to be on the site. Which calls do they feel have little value?
- Work with your marketing team and legal department to make sure the information you want to put on your site is acceptable for public consumption. You don't want to give your competitors an advantage. For instance, when I was in the boat business, we would only allow parts manuals on the site for boats that were 2 years old or more. We didn't want our competitors to have easy access to all the new parts we may be using in new models. Yes, they could still find a way to get those part names, but at least they would have to work a little harder, especially for the hard to see parts.
- This information helps your dealers as well, particularly if you have vintage product. A customer who is refurbishing an old product can occupy a lot of time asking the dealer's service department to look up old parts and research information with no payback.
- By all means survey your dealers and customers and ask what they would like to see on the site. We used to run contests with our dealers for suggestions. The prize was a $50 gift card. A small price for valuable information.
- If you have a protected website for your dealers, this process works the same way. The information may be more

focused to repair work instructions and flat rates, but dealer self-help is huge as well. Dealers love it when you have detailed work instructions with flat rates on them so they can quickly schedule work with the right technicians.

The main thing is to get started and let the process evolve. Customers will respond with positive feedback if they like what they see. It is all about adding value for the customer and working efficiently for your company.

Tip #9

1. Customer self-service can save your company time and money! The customer will also love you for all the information they can find on your products.
2. Customers would rather use information from your website vs. third-party sites.

10.

2%/100% Rule

I developed the "2%/100%" rule years ago when I was in the marine business. I went through a stretch of time when I was feeling frustrated because of product issues. We were getting beat up all day every day by customers about how bad our product was because of these issues.

I slipped into the rut of thinking "Can our company make any product that doesn't have any issues so we can have happy customers?" It didn't appear that we could with the number of calls we were taking from customers and dealers about ongoing issues. It made it especially difficult because our boats used third-party equipment such as engines and generators that we did not hold the warranty for. So the customer and dealer had to potentially deal with multiple companies if they had an issue with the boat. It was frustrating for all parties involved!

I felt discouraged for a month or so until I got a chance to visit a city that happened to be by the water. As we were waiting to be called to our seats at a restaurant, I wandered outside and was standing by an inlet sea wall where boats, mostly yachts and sport yachts, were constantly passing. As I observed the line of boats passing by, I noticed that about 80% of the boats cruising by were ours. The light bulb finally went off to the fact that we had a huge customer following with many happy customers that enjoyed and were very proud of their boats.

I realized the disgruntled people we were dealing with were about 2% of our population and customer service dealt with them 100% of the time. 98% of our customers were quite happy; hence our company was growing at a rapid pace. I tried the slogan out on my employees to see their reaction. They started telling me of their experiences when being out at a marina or beach. Many had also gone on customer trips to listen to the comments of our customers.

People told our employees how they loved our product and were satisfied with how we took care of them even if they had issues. This is why they kept coming back.

After that day, I found this slogan to be a great motivator for my teams. When you are in the middle of a field issue or product problem, even though customers are not happy about the issue, they will keep coming back if you take care of it properly.

A positive attitude and working to keep things in perspective will rub off on your teams and they will enjoy their work more. Another critical item is that you can't take a customer's rage personally. As hard as it is, you have to let it bounce off or roll off your back. The customer will only get angrier if you get angry with them. You have to show empathy for the customer and work through the situation.

When you are feeling that nothing is going right, think about the happy customers that you have talked to in the past and why they use your product. There is a reason why they buy your product and keep coming back. Much of this has to do with your employees taking care of them when they have an issue. It has long been proven that if a customer has an issue and it is resolved in a positive manner, they will be even more loyal than a customer that has never had a problem.

It is just as we have discussed in earlier chapters; when issues arise, give your customers options and make their satisfaction a priority. Great companies succeed not because they never have issues, but because they don't let the issues get the best of them.

Remember as well, there is a portion of the 2% of unhappy customers that you may never please no matter what you do. All you can do is offer them reasonable options and let the customer make the choice if they are going to be happy or not.

This rule sounds so easy, but it will help get you out of a rut and let you get back in the game to make a difference. Customer service, technical support and many of the other support services specialize in helping people that are not happy. The quicker you realize this, the quicker you are going to have a happier customer who will buy more of your product.

Tip #10

Customers buy your product because they like your product more than your competitors. If you are in a rut because of current product issues, here are a few things you can do to get back on a positive track:

1. Save customer thank you letters and read them when you are not feeling your best about what you are doing.
2. Have your employees submit positive customer interactions and share them with your team.
3. Get out to a customer event to see positive customer interactions so you can see what they like about your product.

"Celebrate small victories to drive Momentum!"

11.

Connected at all Levels and Departments of the Organization

Getting connected at all levels doesn't mean brown-nosing executive management or being the company clown while keeping the troops happy. It simply means figuring out who throughout the organization can help you succeed. It also means helping your teams become more effective by taking road blocks out of their way. Your job is not to run the supervisor's or manager's departments, but to help them get through the red tape to get projects on the map and completed. I typically find that there are a handful of people that become your go-to people when something is needed.

When you come into a company at middle- to senior-level management, the employees assume you know what you are doing. Much of knowing what you are doing is finding the people within the organization that can help you accomplish the tasks to reach the goals. All of the companies I have joined have been new industries for me. I had no preconceived idea about how the industry worked or who the players were within the company or the industry itself. It doesn't take long to figure out the players within your company after you observe for a few weeks.

One of the things that has always worked for me is admitting that I did not know the particular process (let's say how to build a boat) so I was always willing to learn from the front line employees. I would let them tell me their job and how they accomplished it. This would give me a contact in that department if I needed it in the future. Being in customer service, you typically need to interact with multiple departments to resolve a customer issue. Being willing to listen to an employee tell you what they do for a living gives the employee a chance to boast about how good they are at their job and what skills they have that makes them the best. Whether they are the best or not is not important, you will decide that as you get to know all the employees.

Get to know the people in the critical departments such as shipping, accounting, purchasing and any others that may assist in expediting requests. The people in these departments can save you many times over when things are tough and you need help. When I go into a new company, I like to walk around and introduce myself to all these folks so they know who I am and what I do. These people usually get little recognition, and when they do it is for the wrong reason. Make it a point to say hello and thank them for helping you out no matter how small the task is that they helped you with. It will pay off.

Many managers are very good at what they do, but do not develop relationships with other departments. They then struggle because they haven't created working relationships with other departments, or worse yet, they treat them like second-class citizens. One way to crack the code is to volunteer to sit on a committee so you can meet different people and find out who makes things happen. It may take a little time, but you will start to notice who the movers and shakers are and who just talks a lot.

You will become a valued member of the team more quickly by spending the time to get to know people. Try hard to remember names after the first meeting and call them by name when speaking with them.

I get asked frequently how I'm able to get things done so quickly, especially things some people would deem to be nearly impossible to accomplish. It is not easy, but if you have the right connections to get the road blocks out of the way, you get it done because you have a team of people working towards the same goal and you are not doing it by yourself. I freely admit to people that I didn't do it - a team of people did it. Give other departments credit for their work and make sure they are recognized for it. Trust me they will work even harder for you the next time.

Another way to get connected is to ask your employees who they think makes things happen around the office and who they respect or go to when they need help. One of the skills many people lack is teamwork. You may get a win or two by yourself, but successful people usually can name many people that have helped them get there. Being humble and willing to learn will make you successful in the long term.

If you have employees in multiple or remote locations, make it a point to call or visit them on a regular basis. If you go visiting, make sure to meet other people at the facility as well so they get to know you and what you do.

Here are a few things to do when going into a new company:

1. Meet with your employees one-on-one (all levels). You will be amazed how much employees appreciate this.
2. Review the department operation and quickly learn which departments impact yours the most. Meet the employees of those departments so they know your goals.
3. Hold quarterly update meetings with your teams to let them know how they are doing. You should celebrate the accomplishments of the quarter. People are astonished at what they have accomplished when you show it to them in a presentation.
4. When you are traveling to other company locations, make it a point to reach out and meet employees that you may only talk with via email or over the phone. They will appreciate that you took the time to find them and say hello.
5. Be willing to learn, and ask questions without being judgmental.
6. Don't over-promise things you can't control. I make it a point to be very clear about not promising or guaranteeing anything unless I have it in my hand.
7. Be willing to do small tasks that are not your responsibility, such as filling the copy machine with paper or picking up trash. Employees notice and appreciate that you don't think those jobs are below you.

Tip #11

Getting connected is not all about being the popular person, it is about being the person that your employees know will stand up for them and go to battle when things get tough or they need help to resolve issues. You can't be afraid to roll up your sleeves and get dirty. It is about bringing value to the company's success by eliminating road blocks that stop projects in their tracks. Be trustworthy and willing to admit when you are wrong. Being humble is a valuable trait!

12.

Catch Them Doing It Right!

Catching employees doing things right seems so obvious, but it is overlooked in many organizations. You hear it time and time again from employees about how supervisors and managers only say something when things go wrong.

Typically if an employee is asked to come to the manager's office, the employee automatically thinks he or she has done something wrong. In many instances, I have had an employee ask "Am I in trouble for something?" before I can even utter a word. This validates the way the employee has been treated over the years. If your company surveys employees, this is always an important topic to address. It is an easy problem to rectify, but you need to make a conscious effort to make it happen.

I had an office once where the customer service department was just outside my door. Any time I had someone in my office and shut the door, people wanted to know what was going on or what the person in my office did wrong. It took me a while to notice it, but I happened to hear an employee asking someone one day about what was going on after I had spoken with an employee about a situation. The situation was with a customer and not the employee. The chatter I heard was "What did Leslie do wrong? Why was she in the boss's office?" I asked the supervisor why people assumed somebody was in trouble if I wanted to talk with them. She told me the last manager only talked to people when they were in trouble. So I started asking other managers how the previous person ran the department and they confirmed the same thing.

First, if you have to discipline an employee you shouldn't be afraid to do it, but this is not the only time you should find time to talk with an employee. Employees like to know when they are doing things well. Many managers feel the employees know when things are going well so they shouldn't have to say it, or they only praise the whole group and not individuals. Praising the group is fine, but human nature says that individuals like to be recognized for their hard work. Try it out and see what happens.

By catching people doing it right, employees quickly know that you are engaged in what they are doing and care about them. Again, this isn't about being popular; it is about noticing positive outcomes in your departments and recognizing the people that are making it happen. You can also solicit others, such as sales people or other departments, to have a positive influence. My groups have always been associated with assisting sales with their job. I routinely have sales people tell me how great my employees are and how they couldn't do their job without them. When I hear that, I always ask if they have told the person or if there is a way to reward the person. I ask the sales person to recommend them for an award if they feel that employee's action deserves it. The smile on an employee's face when they receive something they are not expecting is priceless!

Management by walking around really does work and you should make it part of your routine. You get to know what your employees are doing and who is making an impact on your department. You can also pick up on the dynamics of your department. Who are the players and what gets them excited? If your company has an award program use it to recognize your employees. That's what it is there for. Even if there is not extra money involved with the reward, people will appreciate the thought.

Start today catching people doing things right. You shouldn't have to look hard to find something positive to point out. Start out by recognizing the group and then work your way to the individuals. Once employees know you care, productivity will start to rise and the employees will be happier to come to work.

There are multiple ways to award employees. Here are some that I have used in the past:

- Company awards – Many larger companies have established programs that recognize people for everyday accomplishments as well as big breakthroughs. Use them. If your company doesn't have a program, develop a program yourself for your teams.

- Employee of the month and year. These work well if there are well-defined metrics to go with them. Be careful not to make them a popularity contest.

- Dress-down coupons – Employees love these in my groups. They love the opportunity to dress casual during the week.

- Stop by an employee's desk and thank them for getting a customer issue resolved or for any other task that helps out the department.

- Share positive emails with them when a customer or another employee notes the hard work that has been done by one of your employees. I always forward positive emails to my executive management to let them know when things are going right. This highlights the employee and shows the positive effect we have on our business.

- We have team-building weeks once a quarter to allow employees to get to know one another better and also to recognize the hard work they do on a day-to-day basis. We have popcorn, slushies, and games that encourage people to work together. Friendly competition is always a great motivator.

- If you have the opportunity, recognize an employee during a national sales meeting or publicly at your company. When our employees get on stage to get an award and look out at 200 people clapping, they are proud and excited to continue doing a great job when they return to work.

Tip #12

Catch people doing it right and watch what happens! The impossible quickly becomes possible.

13.

Employee Career Paths – How to Keep Your Employees Growing

"I'm stuck in my current job and there is no career growth in what I do." I hear this every place I have worked and many times it is true. The answer to solving this issue is multi-faceted and not always an easy fix. First, the company has to have the ability or room to help people grow (i.e. growing sales or company expansion). Second, the employee has to keep learning and be willing to take on more responsibility to grow his or her career.

Unless it is a very small company, most provide lots of headroom for entry or midlevel employees. The company needs specific skill sets to continue to stay ahead of the competition and sell more products or services. If an employee doesn't have the right skills, then he or she must be willing to invest in learning new skills to be an asset to the company. This is how people get promoted over time.

One of the biggest stumbling blocks for many employees is that they think just because they have been there for X amount of years they are entitled to get promoted and make more money. This is acutely false in my mind. The company pays them for the job they do, and these days it is very easy to find out if their job skills are being compensated accordingly. Just Google salaries for specific job categories, or go to job websites to see what jobs in a particular discipline are being compensated. Don't be blinded by higher pay because the job is in a high cost region. Look at the national averages. This will give you and your employees a quick assessment of where they are in their career. Many companies have already done this work and the job comes with a salary range that is based on the national average for a category. Don't accept that they should get the promotion because they have been with the company X amount of years. This gets zero points with me. It works if they use it to discuss their accomplishments over those years and what they can add in the future, but it doesn't work if they state that they are owed the position because of their time served.

I have had many employees state that they deserve a raise or promotion because they have been at the company 15 years or have been in the same job for 10 years. My question is always "So what have you done to get yourself out of this job to the next level?" I typically get a strange look and not such a nice response. Remember the company owes the employee a fair wage for the work they do. The employee with the help of their front line managers and supervisors (i.e. YOU) can continue to grow no matter how long they have been at the company if they are willing to work for it.

Take a hard look at your group and what jobs are available within the department. In customer service, technical support and most jobs there are levels. The levels start out for the new employees, and as they grow they can move up within their job discipline without leaving the department. For example, the customer service groups I have managed have had the following positions: Customer Service Representative B (new employee), Customer Service Representative A, Customer Service Senior, Customer Service Lead, Customer Service Supervisor, and Customer Service Manager. If your company doesn't have multiple levels, meet with your HR representative and see if you can create these positions over time. This will help you retain employees long term. With each position comes more responsibility and duties as well as what everyone looks for, more money.

Some things to do for employees:

- Routinely ask your employees what their ambitions and goals are. Not every employee wants to be the manager of the department.
- Constantly remind your employees that they need to continue to grow so the company can stay in the lead and beat the competition.
- Evaluate where your employees are salary-wise so you can speak intelligently about their pay if asked. If they are

being severely underpaid, work with HR to gradually reward employees that deserve a raise. I have done this many times and morale has improved greatly because they know I'm watching out for them.

- Look at the available job positions in your departments and see what positions are stepping-stones for your employees so you can encourage them to apply for them if they come available.
- Never try to hold good employees back from improving their skills or moving to a better position. This will only prompt the employee to leave over time. Let's face it; you wouldn't want to be held back!
- Make employee evaluations meaningful. This includes addressing bad habits and areas that need to be improved. The employee may not like it when you talk to them about it, but they will thank you later if it helps them get to a better place over time. I love turn around stories.
- Do evaluations at least once a year so there are no surprises. Don't wait until it is evaluation time to discuss bad habits and poor performance. It will only get you a blank look from the employee or anger.
- Like we discussed in the last chapter – Catch them doing it right!
- Make sure the employee knows that it is up to them to make their career grow and you are there to help, but you can't make it happen for them.
- Empower your employees.

Tip #13

You don't have to be perfect, but you have to care. If your employees are growing and successful you will also be successful and grow to new heights. Take some of your own medicine. You have to continue to learn to make your career grow.

14.

Wrap-Up

Implementing the tips mentioned in the previous chapters is no easy task, and it has taken me years to manage them consistently. The tricky part of all this is the fact that different strategies work depending on your team DNA and the type of business you are in.

Employees respond to managers that are sincere, respectful and have the drive to win. I have had many challenges in my life personally and professionally and I haven't won every battle, but I keep trying new things to find the magic technique that works.

A Navy Commander that I worked for once told me, "Ray, whatever decision you make, do it wisely and never look back" This has worked for me. It doesn't mean you never re-evaluate what your decision was, but it does mean you need to learn from your decisions and keep getting up when you get knocked down. Move forward and don't dwell on the past, which you can't change.

I tell my teams all the time that I'm not bashful about telling executives that I surround myself with people that are smarter than I am! The trick is to take all that brain power & energy and turn it into productivity. Make it a mission to promote your people when they deserve it and help them get to a better place in their career, even if it means you will lose them from your team. This management quality will pay off time and time again. It has for me. I have a strong professional network that is made up of many great friends that I have gone to battle with to make companies successful.

Be one of those leaders who is known for being tough, but fair. I stand by this motto from being in the Navy – "I want to work with people that I would want to go into battle with and win the war." This means I want to work with people that want to win, will listen to the people under them, and will treat them with respect. I expect them to help me grow, and provide guidance and constructive criticism when needed.

Tip #14

A line from a movie I always remember is "Chance favors the prepared mind." (Under Siege II, The Dark Territory). Be prepared and make things happen. Good luck in your professional journey!

"Employees produce for Leaders and maintain for managers!"
"Be a Leader"

About the Author

Ray Roberge is a Customer Service professional who has led "World Class" contact centers and has been recognized for creating first class customer service, warranty and technical support teams for a number of Fortune 100 companies.

He holds an MBA from the University of Tennessee and has more than 20 years of Customer Service experience in multiple industries.

www.ingramcontent.com/pod-product-compliance
Lightning Source LLC
Chambersburg PA
CBHW071816170526
45167CB00003B/1323